MW00737002

Suchitra Sen

A Legend In Her Lifetime

Published in 2002 by

Rupa & Co

7/16, Ansari Road, Daryaganj
New Delhi 110 002

Sales Centres:
Allahabad Bangalore Chandigarh Chennai
Dehradun Hyderabad Jaipur Kathmandu
Kolkata Ludhiana Mumbai Pune

Photographs courtesy: Tarun Gupta, Studio Pics and Subhash Chheda, Datakino
Photographs from *Devdas, Aandhi, Mamta, Bambai ka Babu,* etc.
from Subhash Chheda, Mumbai

Cover & Book Design by
Arrt Creations
45 Nehru Apts, Kalkaji, New Delhi 110 019

Printed in India by
International Print-O-Pac Ltd.
Okhla Industrial Area, Phase-I
New Delhi - 110020

Suchitra Sen

A Legend In Her Lifetime

Shoma A. Chatterji

Rupa & Co

CONTENTS

Introduction

Suchitra Sen is the most charismatic actress Bengali cinema has ever seen. Her ethereal beauty, coupled with her phenomenal acting and immense box office popularity, particularly her on-screen pairing with the late Uttam Kumar, has given her legendary cult status in Bengal. She created a new image in Bengali cinema. It was an image that evolved over time. From a beautiful face ideal for the celluloid close-up in black-and-white, shot with chiaroscuro light effects, she graduated to the silent victim of circumstance or love or both. She then transcended these celluloid stereotypes to become the articulate and tragic actress who capitalised on her tragedy. The tragedy was two-fold—it was drawn from personal life and from the characters she portrayed. Within cinema, she was the star-actress, no one could hold a candle to.

As a woman, she broke many rules in the book of the Indian woman stereotype.

Her debut was in the unreleased *Shesh Kothai* in 1952. The following year saw her act opposite Uttam Kumar for the first time in *Saarey Chuattar*. The film, an effervescent comedy was also the breakthrough film of director Nirmal Dey. It was a reasonable hit at the box-office. However it is remembered more for launching the pair of Uttam Kumar and Suchitra Sèn. They went on to become icons of Bengali romantic melodramas for more than twenty years, creating a distinct genre. Their films were famous for the soft-focus close ups of the stars particularly Sen, lavishly mounted scenes of romance against windswept expanses and richly decorated interiors with fluttering curtains and such mnemonic objects as bunches of tube roses.

Suchitra never remained static as an actress. With newer roles, her multi-faceted talent bloomed in different ways. "She is the face that launched umpteen hits. She was a rage, the kind that only Marilyn Montroe became in Hollywood," a film critic had once surmised. But she is more often compared with the great Greta Garbo in the sense that like the famous Garbo persona, no one except her immediate family members, consisting of daughter Moon Moon, son-in-law Bharat Dev Burman and grand daughters Ria

The mellowed beauty in Datta

and Raima, has seen Suchitra Sen except once or twice, since 1978. She continues to live, safely cocooned within her small island of private sunshine, surrounded by her daughter and two granddaughters. She lives in a spacious and beautifully appointed apartment at Ballygunje Circular Road, an elitist pocket in the southern part of Calcutta. The apartment is one of the four she acquired when promoters brought down her original home in the same location to build a series of high-rise apartments. The three other apartments she has bequeathed to her daughter and granddaughters.

Chapter One

From Roma to Suchitra Sen

How did Roma become Suchitra Sen? Suchitra Sen was encouraged by her husband Dibanath to step into films. The story goes that in 1952, she was initially taken for a singing assignment at a recording studio in Park Street. She was introduced as Roma Sen then. But the singing job was shelved in favour of the female lead in a film to be directed by Sukumar Dasgupta, a noted filmmaker of the time. Dasgupta took a screen test. The film was *Saat Number Koyedi*. One of his assistants, Nitish Roy (not to be confused with

The independent doctor in Hospital

Mumbai-based production designer Nitish Roy) re-christened this new actress with a new name—Suchitra.

She signed three more films during the same year. One was *Kajori* directed by Niren Lahiri, then there was *Saare Chuattar* directed by Nirmal De and *Bhagawan Sri Krishna Chaitanya* directed by Debaki Bose in which Basanta Choudhury made his debut in the title role. Her hero in *Saat Number Koyedi* was Samar Roy. Her male counterpart in *Saare Chuattar* was Uttam Kumar.

The number of people in the industry who could call her Roma could be counted on one's fingers. Uttam Kumar was one of them. Among the few others were producer and distributor Asit Choudhury, and Anil Bandopadhyay who was the DCP of Calcutta then. These three friends were influential in Mrs. Sen's life and career. Till date, everyone in the Bengali film industry refers to her either as 'Madam' or as 'Mrs. Sen'. From the outset, she had a reserve about her that wrapped her like an aura, automatically vesting her with a dignified distance not usually seen or recognised in film stars those days, particularly in the actresses.

There was one group that addressed her as 'Sir.' Filmmaker Gulzar who directed Suchitra Sen for *Aandhi* leads the group. He still addresses her as 'Sir' in a military tone of voice and this has remained a mutual joke between them since the making of *Aandhi.* "Though I was much junior to her in experience and in age when she was working in *Aandhi,* she insisted on addressing me as 'Sir'. We went on location with Raakhee and Meghna, who was then a toddler. She became friends with Raakhee but continued to call me 'Sir'. Then, one day, I warned her that if she did not stop calling me 'Sir,' then my entire unit would address her not as 'Madam' but as 'Sir.' This form of address continues between us till this day," reminisces Gulzar.

'Aandhi' one of her last screen appearances

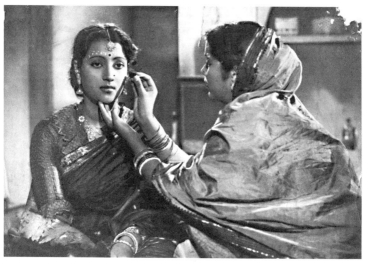

The bride in Devdas

Suchitra Sen's childhood is shrouded in mystery. Some say she studied in Santi Niketan. She grew up in distant Pabna, miles away from Bolpur in Birbhum district, in West Bengal. During her time, daughters of middle-class Bengali families did not go to boarding school. But then, her maternal uncle B.N. Sen lived in Bolpur with his family and she would often come to stay with them. For some time during her early childhood, she lived with her maternal uncle's family in Patna. She was born in Pabna (now in Bangladesh), on April 6. She was the fifth among three brothers and five sisters.

Her father's name was Karunamoy Dasgupta and her mother's name was Indira. Her nickname was Krishna. When she was admitted to the Pabna Girls High School, her father entered Roma as her name in the admission form. She was noted for her beauty right from the time she was a child. In 1947, it was perhaps her beauty that heralded an early marriage to Dibanath Sen, son of an extended joint family that migrated to Calcutta. Suchitra is perhaps the first Indian actress in Bengal to have made her film debut after marriage and motherhood. The year of her birth is somewhat clouded because some sources trace it back to 1931 while others say the year was 1934. This is a part of the mystique that adds to the enigma called Suchirta Sen. In a nostalgia piece penned by journalist Amitabh Choudhury (*Television,* February 1992,) Suchitra Sen is quoted recalling an interesting anecdote from her childhood.

Listen to this incident from my childhood. I was in Patna, staying with my Mama's family. I was about three then, playing in the field, clad only in a pair of tiny panties. A naga sanyasi arrived at my Mama's house. Some time later, I was summoned to show myself to this sanyasi. The man kept staring at me for a long time. Then he said,—this girl will become famous when she grows up. Her name will become a household word. I do not know whether you will believe this. But it is true.

Phoolrani Kannjilal (nee Choudhury) says, "We formed a group of five girls chirping away merrily during the school recess." Phoolrani was Suchitra Sen's classmate at Pabna Girls High School.

"I met her when I changed schools to quit Mahakali Pathshala to join Pabna Girls High School in Class IV. She was already a student there. We would take active part in the cultural programmes of the school. Though she was never very good at studies, she wrote a beautiful hand and was quite conscious about her appearance, her hair plaited down just so, her saree pleated right, always prim and proper in school or at home," says Mrs. Kanjilal. Roma enjoyed dressing up for marriage functions and drew a lot of male attention. But she did not respond, as those were times when free mixing was looked down upon. She recalls Roma teaching girls to dance to the lines of a popular Tagore song that went, *"hriday amaar naacherey aajike, moyurero moto naacherey."* Kanjilal and Roma studied together in the same class for six years. "She was warm and friendly, a girl with good taste and decent manners. No sign of the famous Suchitra Sen 'moods' when she became a star, was evident then," says Kanjilal. "But there was something different about her, something we could not quite put our finger on but could feel. So, when I saw her after a long time on screen and realised that Suchitra Sen was none other than my school friend

Roma, it was not as big a surprise as it ought to have been."

"The biggest surprise during our school days was when Roma came back from a holiday in Puri, a seaside resort in Orissa, where she had gone with her grandmother, and declared, 'my marriage has been fixed.' The boy was Dibanath Sen, son of Adinath Sen, Bar-at-law, who lived in Calcutta. The groom's family placed no demands for dowry—unthinkable in those days—and Roma got married to Dibanath in 1947. "I attended her marriage. She looked beautiful as a bride and contrary to convention, did not cover her

A captivating shot from Devdas

SUCHITRA SEN

head with the bridal veil," reminisces Kanjilal. "But my introduction to Suchitra Sen, the star was in 1954, in the newly released film called *Ora Thaake Odhaare* (They Live on the Other Side). I did not recognise her at once, though. I found a strong resemblance between the actress who played the female lead and my classmate Roma. My sisters echoed my feelings. We asked one of our older brothers who was a technician in Bengali films. He confirmed that Suchitra Sen and my classmate Roma was one and the same person. I could not believe my ears. Several years later, when I saw her with Uttam Kumar in the film *Saarery Chuattar* (74-and-a-half), much after the film was first released, I noticed that her bridal make-up and attire was a celluloid replication of her own marriage," sums up Kanjilal.

"We did meet many years later, in the late sixties. Roma had invited me to her Ballygunje Place home through an actor we both knew well. Parijat Bose, the actor, said he would pick me up and take me to her home. I found two watchmen guarding the entrance. One of them asked me to fill in a slip. But before I could fill it, Roma came down herself and gave me a big hug. She refused to let Parijat leave without taking some sweets because, 'you have brought back an old friend of mine,' she said with her magic smile. She wore no make-up and was draped in an ordinary cotton saree.

The confused doctor in Hospital

It was some time after her film *Fariyaad* was released and she had cut her hair short, I noticed. We exchanged nostalgic memories about our childhood and she expressed a wish to meet the other three girls of our gang—Moloya, Reba and Rekha. When I expressed a desire to watch her shoot for a film, she refused. She said, 'if you once watch the shooting of a film, *any* film, you will lose all the charm of watching a film.' I went there a couple of times more because she had already told me that I needn't call before visiting.

As Parvati in Bimal Roy's Devdas

But then I stopped, because our worlds were too different, and though she was always warm, I felt neither of us had anything more to contribute to our relationship, or the need to sustain it," said Kanjilal.

Dibanath is said to have noticed his wife's artistic potential as soon as they were married. Being culturally inclined, he wished his wife to be a part of the cultural world. His father Adinath Sen's first wife was Bimal Roy's sister. Though the sister passed away quite early and Adinath married again, the family continued to keep links with Bimal Roy and the children continued to address him as "mama." This link came in handy when Dibanath wished to introduce his wife into films. This led to the recording studio event and finally, to *Saat Number Koyedi*. Before shooting was to begin, a big hurdle had to be crossed. Who would talk to Adinath Sen and ask for permission for his daughter-in-law to act in films? Dibanath did not have the courage to approach his father. So Roma took courage in her hands, approached her father-in-law and told him everything. "If you have the talent, I have no right to destroy it. So, if you wish, I will not stop you from fulfilling your dream."

Much later on in her career, when she was the most sought after star-actress in Bengal, Suchitra Sen's marriage ran into stormy

With Dilip Kumar in Devdas

weather till the couple finally decided to part, with Suchitra taking the responsibility of daughter Moon Moon. A few years after the separation—one is not sure if they had divorced—Dibanath Sen passed away in the US where he was working for a merchant shipping company. Moon Moon woke up from a nightmare the day before. On the morning of November 28, 1969, a long-distance telephone call informed Suchitra Sen of the untimely and tragic death of her husband in an accident. Suchitra Sen insisted on having his body flown down to Calcutta to allow Moon Moon have a final glimpse of a father she loved very much. Producers and directors who were close to her and had worked with her during this phase, say that she purged her inner pain by giving of herself totally to her work and this brought out the best of her hidden talents. No one ever heard her pouring her heart out over her personal problems while she was working. A slice of reality was revealed in the way she portrayed the role of Archana in *Saat Paake Baandha*. This was the time when the trouble in her married life had reached a peak.

The screen mother

With Ashok Kumar in Hospital

Dhiren Deb, known to be Suchitra Sen's personal photographer (a label he refuses to acknowledge) during the entire course of her career, knew her well. He has some of the rarest collection of photographs of Suchitra in her private and personal moments. For instance, there is one picture of Suchitra sitting on her haunches, her face split in an ear-to-ear grin, saree jacked up to the knees, chopping fruits for a *pooja* in her home. Another one shows the actress with little Moon Moon wearing a frock, standing by her side. Dhiren Deb is on the other side. The backdrop shows a small

Dakota from which the trio has just landed at Santa Cruz airport to report for the shooting of Bimal Roy's *Devdas*. "The date was June 2, 1955 and at the time, there were no direct flights from Calcutta to Mumbai. We had to change aircraft at Nagpur and it took around seven hours to reach Mumbai," informed Deb. "We were in the same flight for different reasons though. She was reporting for work on *Devdas* and I was on my professional assignment as photographer. Our relationship reached far beyond the constraints of the normal photographer-subject relationship. But the entire credit for this friendship, goes to Madam alone. In all these years

With Soumitra Chatterjee in Saat Paake Bandha

A look — worth a thousand words

of my life as a still photographer in films, I have never met a woman more decent, warmer, more beautiful, more complete and ideal than Madam. Her outstanding personality finds no comparison with any star-actress in the country. I have taken photographs of Suchitra Sen right through her career in films. No photographer, press or otherwise, was permitted on her sets during a shooting. She is one of the most dedicated artistes of Indian cinema. She would report to the studio at least five minutes before the reporting time for shooting, so punctual was she. In my opinion, it is this dedication that makes her reign supreme as the queen of Bengali cinema more than twenty years after she called it a day."

"Suchitra Sen is one of the most loving, warm and friendly women I have met," said Gulzar, recalling his interaction with the star-actress during the making of *Aandhi,* which he directed. Gulzar and Suchitra developed a lasting friendship during the shooting of the film. "I never knew she had noticed and remembered that I like a glass of cold milk every morning. There was not a single occasion when she forgot to give me a glass of cold milk each time I went to visit her at her residence in Calcutta. Once, I had gone on a very short trip and was staying at the Grand. I could not make the time to meet her. Then, Barin-da, (Barin Dhar) a close associate of Suchitra who was married to her younger sister Runa,

came up to my room and said that 'Sir' was waiting for me in the car in the parking lot downstairs. I rushed down to meet her. 'How can you leave without taking your glass of cold milk?' she asked. She took me home and did not allow me to leave until I had taken that glass of cold milk she served me herself. She is a lovely human being with a fine sense of humour. I believe she has the right to choose her friends. She is very hospitable too, and if in spite of all this, she chooses to guard her privacy, I don't think there is anything wrong in that."

Another interesting anecdote he shares is that Suchitra Sen had the rather unusual habit of feeding crumbs to crows out of her own hands. "Feeding pigeons or parrots is a usual sight. One does not usually see *crows* being fed by people. But Suchitra Sen had this fondness for feeding crows. I have seen a crow perch on her shoulder, then clamber down near her hand, and she would feed crumbs to the crow with her own hand," said Gulzar.

Chapter Two

Retirement and Ramkrishna Paramhamsa

Soon after the release of her last film, *Pronoy Pasha* opposite Soumitro Chattopadhyay in 1978, Suchitra Sen withdrew completely from films and public life. She made herself unavailable for interviews, photo-sessions, and new films. She did not attend parties and stopped seeing people other than very close friends. Producers still wished to make her sign on the dotted line. Directors waited for one sign from her to say 'yes' to a role. But she remained, and still remains away from the public eye.

Sri Ramkrishna

No one knows what instigated this strange decision. Because she did not ever give anyone the chance to find out. Her mind turned to spiritualism and she took *deeksha* from Swami Bireshwaranandaji, then President of the Ramkrishna Math and Ramkrishna Mission. She also developed a close bonding with Bharat Maharaj. She looked up to him as a father figure and when he passed away, she was so heart broken that she could not talk properly even to her own family. She began to pay regular visits to the Ramkrishna Math at Belur, and to the Dakshineswar temple. Suchitra Sen also visited another branch of the Ramkrishna Mission at Aantpur in Hooghly district. Aantpur is where Naren, one of Sree Ramkrishna's closest disciples, took to *sanyas*. Ramkrishna Paramhamsa gave him the name Swami Vivekananda. Suchitra felt a strange attraction towards this place. She would often drive down to Aantpur—an hour's drive from the city, to spend the day in this natural ambience like any ordinary woman. She would sit at the feet of the *sanyasis* and listen to their recitation and chants from religious books. Then, she would sit on the floor along with them and partake of the *prasad* after the recital.

Once, during this period of seclusion, noted author Kana Bosu-Misra called her up at her residence. "They are telecasting *Deep Jweley Jai* on the small screen right now," she informed. "What a

Dakshineshwar Temple, Kolkata

brilliant performance you have given in the film," she added. The voice at the other end of the line kept quiet for a few moments, then said, "That is actress Suchitra Sen, that is not me at all. The Suchitra Sen in screen and this Suchitra Sen talking to you over the telephone are two different people. I did all that once upon a time for my bread and butter. I do not reflect on those days any longer. Today, my entire world is filled with thoughts of Thakur (Ramkrishna)."

Another anecdote on the actress states that once, a close friend of hers informed her that a newspaper report had said that Ramkrishna Paramhamsa was said to have been re-born in the home of a rickshaw puller in Konnagar, a small town some kilometers away from the city. The minute she heard this, she took this director friend along and at the unearthly hour of three in the night they drove to Konnagar to see the newborn. She spent a few hours at the modest home of the rickshaw puller and then came home, finally at peace with herself. Having learnt that Ramkrishna was fond of *jalebis,* Suchitra Sen offers *jalebis* to Thakur Ramkrishna during her daily *pooja.* After the *pooja* is over, she touches the *jalebi* to her forehead and then puts a bit into her mouth.

Sri Ramkrishna Math at Belur

Once, Suchitra Sen requested playback singer Sandhya Mukherjee, whose playback singing played a significant role in Suchitra Sen's films, to come along with the actress to Belur Math. Sandhya Mukerjee says, "She had learnt from Bharat Maharaj that he was a fan of my songs, specially the *bhajans* I had recorded. Suchitra called me up and asked me to go along to meet Bharat Maharaj because he wanted to see me. I agreed at once. I asked her if I could take my husband along. She said yes. All along the drive to

Belur Math, we had a long chat, about our respective families, household matters and such mundane things. Neither her films nor my songs was a part of our conversation that day."

"The way she has withdrawn so completely from public life and space is amazing," says Madhabi Mukerjee, one of Bengal's finest actresses. "This self-imposed seclusion within the four walls of the home year after year—it's been more than two decades now—is not easily achieved. It calls for tremendous determination and will power. She willingly gave up the joys and pleasures of the world beyond the four walls of her home. She had to resist many earthly temptations to achieve this. I just cannot bring myself to believe this entire thing. This is penance... Suchitra Sen defines an era. It is an era she herself built, brick by painful brick. It was an era whose magnetic charisma no one could ignore. Till today, she remains a topic of discussion among us. She still occupies an important space within the Bengali psyche."

Only twice did Suchitra Sen emerge from her cocoon of fiercely guarded private space to come before public view. One of these was on 24th July 1980, when Uttam Kumar's body lay in state, awaiting cremation. She stepped out of her car, approached Uttam Kumar's body, garlanded it with flowers, stared at his peaceful face for a few moments, and then quickly stepped back to her car to go home. In 1982, during the Filmotsav in Calcutta, Suchitra Sen would sometimes come to watch an occasional film. She tried to remain incognito behind her signature sunglasses. But these too, were part of her persona and people knew who was wearing them. She also stood by the bedside of her *deeksha* guru Bharat Maharaj when he passed away. His death seemed to shatter her completely for some time.

CHAPTER THREE

The Evolution of an Actress

The rise of Suchitra Sen from a beautiful face may be classified into three phases, not necessarily in terms of chronology, but in terms of her growth as an actress. A career that began in 1953 with *Saat Number Koyedi* culminated with *Pronoy Pasha*. She retained her charisma as a much-in-demand star-actress in Tollygunje, though she was already into her mid-forties and not all her films were faring well at the box office. She and Uttam Kumar had virtually stopped working with each other after *Priyo Bandhabi* (1974) directed by Hiren Nag, which did not do too well.

In Mamta *as the mother*

In Saat Paake Bandha.
The role fetched her the Best Actress Award at the Moscow Film Festival

The passively beautiful heroine as mere foil to the hero: With or without Uttam Kumar cast opposite her, in her first phase of films, Suchitra Sen was principally a beautiful face with large, almond-shaped eyes, a beautiful mouth, an oval face, a long, graceful neck and lustrous black hair falling all the way down to her waist. She presented the typical Bengali-girl stereotype with her saree draped around her slender frame to reveal the contours of a soft feminine body that appeared more sensuous because it was concealed, a loose lock of hair that fell over her forehead which she moved away with the back of her hand. The role of Sree Chaitanya Mahaprabhu's wife Bishnupriya in *Bhagaban Sri Krishna Chaitanya* was a rather marginal one, which gave her little scope to demonstrate her acting. However, this was one of the few period films Suchitra did in her entire career. She was noticed almost at once both by the audience as well as by filmmakers for her haunting screen presence. The reason lay in the fact that these films were essentially hero-centric and the heroine was a necessary support in his attempts to triumph over life's hurdles. Examples are—*Shaap Mochan, Trijama, Dhuli, Moroner Pawre,* etc. In these films, Suchitra Sen was either too subdued to contribute anything significant, or tended to be melodramatic in scenes of intense drama. The other reason is that filmmakers of the time did not explore the

Woman in love — Datta

potential she had, the work she was capable of, which showed up in sudden sparks whenever she was called upon to give of her best and her character was as important as that of the hero. Directors seemed more interested in exploiting her screen persona, her beauty, her box office pull, than trying to tap the talent that lay hidden inside.

Suchitra Sen without Uttam Kumar: Suchitra Sen did not always have the suave and charming presence of Uttam Kumar to bolster her screen presence. Suchitra Sen lit up the silver screen with her electric presence, the myriad subtle expressions flitting in and out of her face, and of course, later in her career, her tremendous talent for understatement. All this led to a terrific box office draw, with or without Uttam, as Suchitra blazed an unbeatable trail as a tragic actress. She could convey more with a look than most actresses. Her tear-filled glistening eyes and husky dialogue delivery could even give that ultimate tragedienne of Indian cinema, Meena Kumari, a run for her money.

Some believe that at a certain stage in her career, Suchitra must have felt that her audience and her critics did not believe she could carry a film alone minus the support of Uttam Kumar. So, as a litmus test of her box office draw, she began acting without

43

Uttam Kumar in heroine-centred films. Cast opposite her were actors much her junior such as Soumitra Chatterjee, Ranjit Mullick besides some peers of Uttam Kumar like Basanta Choudhury and seniors like Bikash Roy and Asit Baran. Did the litmus test prove her point? Of course it did, as if, almost with a vengeance. Notable among these films are—*Deep Jweley Jai, Smriti Tuku Thaak, Sandhya Deeper Shikha, Uttar Phalguni, Saat Paake Bandha, Datta, Debi Choudhurani,* etc. There was one film, *Hospital,* directed by Sushil Majumdar, in which Suchitra Sen played a doctor

The radical woman in Hospital

who revealed rare courage by becoming an unwed mother when her lover, a senior doctor (Ashok Kumar) refused to marry her. Some Bengali directors owe their best films to Suchitra Sen. Among them is the late Asit Sen who would always be associated with two landmark films—*Deep Jweley Jai* and *Uttar Falguni.*

In *Deep Jweley Jai,* Suchitra played Radha, a hospital nurse employed by a progressive psychiatrist, Pahari Sanyal. She is trained to develop an emotional relationship with male patients as part of therapy. Sanyal diagnoses the hero, Basanta Choudhury, as suffering from trauma after being rejected by the woman he loved. The psychiatrist orders Radha to play the role of the lover. She is hesitant to begin with because an earlier case left her emotionally involved with the patient who forgets her when he was cured, leaving her behind to nurse her wounds in silence. But Sanyal insists and Radha agrees, only to fall in love all over again. When the new patient is completely cured of his trauma, it is Radha who withdraws into a world of her own, losing her sanity in the process. The film is filled with beautiful, often partly lit close ups of Suchitra Sen which set the tone of the film. Suchitra's performance in the film— her slow transition from a balanced and emotionally hurt woman who tries to place her profession before her emotion, to a woman deeply in love with her patient, to the nurse who can no longer recognise the difference between nursing and loving—was hypnotic.

Uttar Falguni saw Suchitra carrying the film on her shoulders in the double role of mother and daughter. The mother is forced to turn into a *thumri* singing courtesan who turns the care and upbringing of her daughter to the man who loved her. The daughter grows up to be an emancipated barrister. Initially, the daughter reveals her disgust when her 'uncle' takes up the 'dirty' case of a courtesan who has killed her own husband. When she learns that the courtesan is her own mother, she takes on the defence. The film makes extensive use of Asit Sen's characteristic panning shots and lap dissolves as narrative bridges particularly in the sequence of the daughter growing up. Sen remade the film in Hindi as *Mamta* again starring Suchitra.

In *Saat Paake Bandha,* directed by Ajoy Kar, Suchitra was paired with Soumitra Chatterjee. She portrayed Archana, a brilliant girl from an affluent family who falls in love with her professor. Though the father approves of the match, the mother does not. After the marriage. Archana's mother's interference in her married life creates a crisis of loyalty in Archana. Her husband fails to recognise it and after a string of misunderstandings, they divorce. Archana never

With Soumitra Chatterjee in Saat Paake Bandha

forgives her mother for having broken up her marriage. But her own life turns into one of loneliness and repentance. Her sterling performance brought her the Best Actress Award from the Moscow Film Festival. The evolution and metamorphosis of Archana— physical, social, emotional, psychological—over the span of the film which sees her grow from a young college girl to a mature teacher separated from a husband she loved deeply, appears to be a celluloid reflection of Suchitra Sen's own evolution and metamorphosis as an actress.

Datta was based on a classic by Sarat Chandra Chattopadhyay. Contrary to the heroines of his other novels that often revolve around a male character, *Datta* was even *titled* after the heroine— her name was Bijoya. This is one of his few literary works Sarat Chandra converted into a play named *Bijoya*. Suchitra Sen carried the character on her able shoulders, paired as she was, opposite a much younger Soumitra Chatterjee—the dedicated village doctor Naren she falls hopelessly in love with. By this time, Suchitra Sen's personality had acquired a dignity and an aura of the regal not seen in Bengali cinema till today. She made full use of this personality trait to invest the character of Bijoya with dignity. The screen Bijoya in *Datta* portrayed by Suchitra Sen rose above the literary character Sarat Chandra created in his novel. Suchitra

In Bambai ka Babu *with Dev Anand*

achieved this without having to distort the original in any way.

Suchitra Sen and Hindi Cinema: Musafir, Devdas, Champakali, Sarhad, Bambai Ka Babu, Mamta and *Aandhi* are the seven films that go to complete Suchitra Sen's love affair with Hindi films. Beginning with Bimal Roy's *Devdas* in 1955, she went on to act in four more films in quick succession. These were—*Musafir* and *Champakali* (1960) and *Bambai Ka Babu* and *Sarhad* (1960.) She came back to act in the Hindi version of a Bengali hit, (Uttar

Datta

Phalguni) *Mamta* in 1966. Gulzar decided to direct her in one of the most memorable roles of her career in *Aandhi* in 1974. Though her Hindi diction was really bad, and she was almost a stranger to the Hindi audience, her voice was never dubbed and was retained in its originality in every film. She had a different director for each of these films and a wide variety of roles in terms of characterisation. From Parvati in *Devdas,* she went on to play the female lead in one of the three segments of *Musafir,* which marked the directorial debut of Hrishikesh Mukherjee, a noted editor of films.

Suchitra Sen's ouevre of Hindi films is characterised by her acting opposite three generations of Hindi actors. From Dilip Kumar in *Devdas,* she acted with Shekhar, who was senior to Dilip Kumar, in *Musafir.* Bharat Bhushan, another senior actor, played her romantic opposite in *Champakali* while in two films, *Bambai Ka Babu* and *Sarhad,* then heart-throb Dev Anand was her hero. *Mamta* saw her portray the dual role of mother and daughter. While Ashok Kumar portrayed the role of the mother's devoted love, the young, up-and-coming Dharmendra was the man the younger Suchitra Sen fell in love with. Sanjeev Kumar had his dream realised when he played her estranged husband in *Aandhi*. The directors too, represented a wide range in terms of experience, fame, talent and commercial success. In chronological order, they are—Bimal Roy (*Devdas*), Hrishikesh Mukherjee (*Musafir*), Nandlal Jaswantlal (*Champakali*), Raj Khosla (*Bambai ka Babu*), Shankar Mukherjee (*Sarhad*), Asit Sen (*Mamta*) and Gulzar (*Aandhi*).

Bambai ka Babu

Bimal Roy had originally approached Meena Kumari to portray Parvati. She had to refuse for want of the dates Roy needed. The next choice was Madhubala. But Dilip Kumar nixed Madhubala because they were not on good terms. So, Suchitra Sen turned out to be the next choice. This time, it worked. However, the name of Suchitra Sen in the banners and posters of a Hindi film failed to repeat the Calcutta magic at the box office. If *Mamta* clicked, it was mainly because of its rich musical score and the melodious songs. Dilip Kumar admired her work in *Devdas*. "Suchitra Sen is a great artiste," he once said. "For the first time, in her, I came across an ideal blend of beauty and brains in a single woman. She is extra-ordinary. She was interested in things beyond the world of cinema. I have deep respect for her because of the total dedication and seriousness with which she approached her work during the making of a film."

Hrishikesh Mukherjee recalled that when he was making his directorial debut, he was a bit uncertain about how established stars of Bombay would respond to his call to act in his film. "Roma had no such hang-ups. I had seen her work in some Bengali films, and of course watched her work in person in Bimal-da's *Devdas*. This made me decide to take her in one of the three story segments in *Musafir*. We had already evolved a sweet brother-sister relationship during the making of *Devdas*. She accepted the

Bambai ka Babu

proposal at once and quoted a sum so much lower than her market rate that I could not believe my ears," said Hrishikesh Mukherjee. Though the film did not do well at the box office, the relationship between the two remained the same. "Had she gone on doing Hindi films, she could have taken far longer strides in her career than she ultimately did. But then, Bengali cinema did not afford her with the time and space she needed for Hindi films." She had a few mannerisms like holding on a particular expression for a time longer than needed for a given shot, or, looking at her co-

With Ashok Kumar in Hospital

actor in a particular way, which limited her range as an actress. "But then, she might have deliberately held on to them believing they added to her screen magnetism," added Hrishi-da. May be they did.

The only Hindi film that best underscored Suchitra Sen's unique command over histrionics was Gulzar's *Aandhi*. "I loved her work in *Aandhi*," said Dev Anand who acted with Suchitra in two films. "Though she is a bit inclined to over-act, among her contemporaries in Indian cinema, Suchitra has no peer in the field of acting."

Gulzar remembers "The proposal for a film pairing Suchitra Sen with Sanjeev Kumar came to me from J. Om Prakash. There was this script penned by Sachin Bhowmik. Since I did not like it, Sachin-da asked me for some more time to re-work the script. I then started writing a story about a woman politician and an hotelier. While the story got written, writer Kamleshwar had a story of his own which he wished to show to one Mr. Dhoondhi in the south. He wanted to take me along as he wished me to direct the film. But Dhoondhi rejected Kamleshwar's story and liked the one I had written. Kamleshwar wrote the novel *Aandhi* based on the film *after* the script was written. I decided to make Kamleshwar a part of my team and *Aandhi* is the result of this team-work."

"Sanjeev Kumar was keen on doing a film opposite Suchitra Sen to be made by Sohanlal Kanwar with me as the writer. At the time, I did not agree to this proposal. Three years later, when I approached Suchitra Sen for the *Aandhi* role, she read the script, smiled and said that she would do it without suggesting any changes whatsoever in the script," said Gulzar. When questioned why, knowing Suchitra's Hindi to be bad, he did not dub her lines, Gulzar says, "I felt she ought to be respected for what she is and her voice is an integral part of what she is. I had no desire to change her voice at any point during or after the making of the

Datta — *the face in the mirror*

film." Gulzar insists that *Aandhi* had nothing to do with the life and career of Indira Gandhi as was commonly believed. "We had to have a *model* on which to build up the character of a woman politician. What better model could we have had other that the one Mrs. Gandhi offered? Suchitra Sen had to give the character a particular image. We decided to invest it with the public image of Indira Gandhi."

CHAPTER FOUR

The Uttam-Suchitra Magic

Suchitra Sen, alongwith Uttam Kumar, formed one of the most enduring romantic screen pairs in the history of cinema. At their best, the pair made the likes of Raj Kapoor-Nargis, Spencer Tracy-Katherine Hepburn pale in comparison, such was the luminosity and chemistry between them on screen. Together, the Uttam-Suchitra pair heralded the golden age of Bengali cinema.

Historically, these two as a star couple on screen arrived at a critical time when Bengali cinema was going through a bad phase. New

Trial by Fire : Agni Pareeksha

Theatres, that had reigned supreme for many years, gifting Bengali cinema with some of its best actors, such as Pramathesh Barua, Kanan Devi, Pahari Sanyal, technicians like Bimal Roy, Nitin Bose, and music directors like R.C. Boral and Pankaj Mullick, had pulled down its shutters with *Bokul* (1954.) Interestingly, Uttam Kumar had starred in its last two productions. Then Bengali cinema was going through severe marketing troubles, as one of the long-term consequences of the Partition when East Bengal had gone to

Pakistan. There was a conspicuous dearth of new faces and talent and in terms of technique, production values had declined and Bengali cinema was losing its glamour. Finally Hindi films were becoming more popular. Within this rather gray phase, a film called *Agni Pareeksha* introduced a star couple.

Their physical beauty, style of expressing romance on screen and finally, their glamour came like a life-saving drug for an industry gasping for breath. They heralded a spring, a breath of fresh air that lasted more than two decades. Lovers tried to identify with the love they projected on screen. Every member of the audience would wait with bated breath for the typical climax of a Suchitra-Uttam film where the two would get into a close embrace with the THE END sign superimposed on them. In one of these films, *Shilpi,* the hero dies in the end. The film was a flop. During this phase, Uttam Kumar was paired with other actresses also. He acted opposite Sabitri Chatterjee in 27 films. Most of them were commercial hits. But they failed to create the magic Uttam could effect with Suchitra facing him in front of the camera.

The Suchitra-Uttam pairing had another rare quality. The two could change the screen magic of their romance in keeping with the changing needs of a different script or director or role. In their

The magical chemistry of love

earlier phase, the Suchitra-Uttam on-screen romance was noted for the intense passion it generated visually, through dialogue and through imaginatively choreographed song sequences. The love songs lip-synched by them, are big hits in the music industry to this day. For the three film versions of the Sarat Chandra classics they acted in—*Chandranath, Rajlakshmi-O-Sreekanta* and *Grihadaha,* they changed the very definition of romance from the passionate to the subdued, in full control of their emotions.

The two acted together in 30 films spanning two decades. They created between them a distinct *genre* of romance that acquired the label of the Uttam-Suchitra romance. They shared an excellent rapport on the sets though they were never known to have fallen actually in love, despite what the gossip magazines then would often insist. Both began their careers after their marriages. This did nothing to spoil the magic of their box office charisma. Though they appeared together for the first time in *Saare Chuattar,* a rollicking comedy, the film that established the two as a unique box-office pair was *Agni Pareeksha* (Trial by Fire), directed by Bibhuti Laha, released in 1954.

In an interview, Laha said, "When I chose this pair for *Agni Pareeksha,* everyone said I was crazy to have paired a flop master with a dumb doll. These were euphemisms the film industry used for them at the time. The only thing both Uttam and Suchitra had going for them was their face. I concede that it was a considerable risk I took in taking them on to play the two leads in a film that called for considerable acting talent. Till the last minute, everyone tried to make me change my mind and cast Bikash Roy and Anubha Gupta in their place. But I was determined to cast new faces. The film proved to be their starting point. My only credit lies in that I played the first tunes on the flute."

Anup Kumar, the character actor who passed away some years

ago, said, "During the sixties, the entire audience in Bengal was convinced that Uttam Kumar and Suchitra Sen were lovers in real life too. Producers and directors cashed in on this popular notion as much as they could, and almost always with happy results. Young boys and girls would use their names together as 'Uttam-Suchitra,' so complete was their popularity and identification with the masses. I worked with them in many films. While I waited for my shot on the sets, the perfect rapport the two shared, amazed me again and again. Roma-di knew precisely how Uttam-da would respond to what line of dialogue. Uttam-da too, understood her moods completely. This chemistry between them brought out some of the best romantic performances in Bengali cinema. The Uttam-Suchitra pair proved that it was possible to bring cinema right into the streets to touch the man out there. When the girl next door came to hang out the day's washing, the boy from the neighbouring terrace would belt out a song in typical Uttam Kumar style from an Uttam-Suchitra film. This ability to identify so completely with the audience is an extremely difficult task. But these two had turned this near-impossible task into reality. This was backed by the fact that whatever ego-hassles, problems linked to their acting together on screen they might have shared in the course of their professional lives, they never once were rude to each other in public.

Uttam Kumar's younger brother Tarun Kumar, a noted character actor of the Bengali screen, said that to the best of his knowledge, the celluloid romance between his brother and Suchitra Sen never translated into their real lives. "Every actor knows that it is easier to act out what the director says. But it is impossible to reproduce scenes from one's real life. Our lives may be filled with dramatic incidents, but this does not reduce our entire life into a drama. My own theory about the phenomenal popularity of the Uttam Kumar-Suchitra Sen pair is that almost throughout their career together, they shared a spirit of healthy competition and mutual respect. This did not sustain in the later years for many reasons. But even during this time, they never ever slighted each other."

Among the most memorable films co-starring Uttam Kumar and Suchitra Sen are—*Harano Sur* (1957) and *Saptapadi* (1961), both directed by Ajoy Kar. *Harano Sur* was a big hit even in Mumbai where it ran in Sunday morning shows for months at Parel's Ganesh theatre. *Harano Sur* was said to have borrowed the amnesia theme from the Hollywood film *Random Harvest*. The soft, graceful woman in love with her amnesia patient, fully aware of the risks when he gets his memory back is unforgettable in its suggestively emotive potential. She tends to the helpless amnesiac (Uttam Kumar) but loses him when he regains his memory. Though Uttam Kumar was the hero, it was Suchitra Sen who ran away with the audience sympathy and the hearts of all the men in the audience. The song, *tumi je amaar* (you are mine) sung by Gita Dutta in her sensuous voice, enriched both the performance and the characterisation of Roma, the name Suchitra was given in the film. The blend of her beauty and her histrionics crowned with the electric chemistry she created with Uttam Kumar on screen, makes *Harano Sur* a truly unforgettable experience.

Saptapadi was a different cup of tea altogether. In an opinion poll asking them to name their dream role, every contemporary Bengali actress was unanimous in her choice of Rina Brown played by Suchitra Sen in *Saptapadi*. The film was based on a novel by Jnanpeeth awardee Tarasankar Bandopadhyay. For Suchitra Sen specially, it was a solid, author-backed role. The story had strong potential for celluloid melodrama and Ajoy Kar struck the right chord by choosing Uttam Kumar and Suchitra Sen to play the main leads of Krishnendu Mukherjee and Rina Brown. The two characters grow, change, fall in love, part company, and reunite in the most unusual circumstances against the backdrop of World War II, metamorphosing into completely different people towards the closure of the film. Their relationship also changes. While Krishnendu converts to Christianity in order to marry Rina, Rina

The romance and the magic

leaves him and goes away when his father persuades her to leave
him. Krishnendu becomes a priest, and devotes himself to nursing
war victims. When Rina is brought to him as a patient, she is no
more than an over made-up, drunken, Anglo-Indian hired to
entertain the troops at war. Despite her bad English accent, her
loud acting in the opening scenes of the film where she gives
Krishnendu and his friends a bad dressing down, her enacting of
Desdemona for the college staging of Shakespeare's *Othello* where
her lines were dubbed by Jennifer Kapoor, Suchitra Sen rose above

66

the character of Rina Brown and converted her into Suchitra Sen all over again. Desdemona dies in the play, but Rina in the film, phoenix like, rises from her own ashes, saved by Krishnendu and by his deep love for her.

Saptapadi marked the beginning of a break in the Suchitra-Uttam rapport during its making, a crack that widened into a chasm, leading to a clash of two gigantic egos. Half way through the shooting, Suchitra Sen said she would not act in it any more. Uttam Kumar who was the producer, somehow managed to resume shooting and complete the film. It was a super hit. But there were cracks in their then off-screen rapport and this often came across in their post-*Saptapadi* films. This legendary pair could not reproduce the magic screen romance of *Harano Sur, Agni Pareeksha* and *Saptapadi* in films like *Nabaraag, Haar Maana Haar* or *Priyo Bandhobi*. The magic was there, but the glitter had faded, never to shine again.

The Suchitra Sen story remains incomplete without mentioning the gaps in her career. Having redefined the meaning of mainstream cinema for the mass audience, Suchitra Sen never got the chance to work with the three giants of parallel cinema in Bengal, namely, Satyajit Ray, Ritwik Ghatak and Mrinal Sen. Her glamour was so larger-than-life, that somehow, a Suchitra Sen *sans* glamour could never be imagined till Gulzar's *Aandhi*. Satyajit Ray did approach her for the title role in Bankim Chandra's historical fiction *Debi Choudhurani*. She initially agreed but later backed out of the project. "He had asked for dates at a stretch without a break. I could not possibly agree because this would have placed all my other producers in trouble whose films I had either already signed for, or whose films were under production. I could not agree to the exclusivity clause which producer R.D. Bansal later put into the contract," she is reported to have said to journalist Amitabh Choudhuri.

Secondly, Suchitra Sen never acted in a film based on a Tagore classic. She was once chosen to act in a celluloid version of Tagore's classic *Choturango,* to be directed by painter-director Purnendu Pattrea. She had agreed to work for the film because for her, to bring a Tagore character alive on screen was a dream-come-true. But the sudden suicide of Hemen Ganguly, the producer of the film, put paid to all hopes and the film was shelved for good.

The problem with the Suchitra charisma was that once she became the seemingly immortal star in the Bengali cinema horizon, she raised all the characters she portrayed to the level of her own star persona. Her beauty and her stylised performance often came in the way of a complete character-identification. Her acting *appeared* to have shades of Stanislavsky—the ability to go under the skin of the character. But in the ultimate analysis, they all boiled down to one woman—Suchitra Sen. Shades of Bertolt Brecht's distancing the character from the actor could also be seen—because beyond the make-up and the costume and the ambience, it was Suchitra Sen being Suchitra Sen. Perhaps she did this more by design. With her performance in *Aandhi,* she proved how deeply she could imbibe Stanislavky into her system if she wanted to. Perhaps it was commercial cinema's near-total dependence on her star value that drove her to do this.

CHAPTER FIVE

Mother and Grandmother

"I respect and take pride in my mother not only because she entered films when very little technical know-how was available to play tricks with her looks and with her performance, but also because long before the hoo-ha about women's liberation began, she stood for the triumphant woman who won over her male peers," says Moon Moon Sen, actress-daughter of Suchitra Sen. "She brought respectability to her profession at a time when there was little of it to pass around. I respect her because she has defined herself as a legend in her lifetime—something even Uttam Kumar cannot boast of since he is no more." The proud daughter adds that Suchitra Sen was a woman who held herself with dignity throughout her long career spanning several decades. "She has proved that she is a true sophisticate, in the manner in which she gave up her career when she did, proving her unwillingness to be greedy and thus keep the magic intact."

"But she wasn't always like this. Late nights and partying were her forte and she was a party animal," she reminisces. "She loved music, friends and laughter. She had her own circle of friends. Till about ten years ago, she took my daughters out for movies and lunches. She has now distanced herself for personal reasons, reasons I have never questioned." Asked to pick five of her favourites from her mother's oeuvre, Moon Moon promptly tick off *Sandhya Deeper Shikha, Aandhi, Mamta, Saptapadi* and *Saat Pake Bandha*. "I am a bit scared of my daughters' joining films. My mother strangely, has no such qualms so far as the grandchildren are concerned. She does not comment even on their partying all night. She allows them complete freedom and will not entertain any complaints against them. She adores them and even tries cooking for us at times though she is a terrible cook!" smiles Moon Moon.

"My mother spared us the humiliation of watching her being walked all over the screen by youngsters less talented and less able than she was. She lived life without excess, always uninvolved, always exclusive, always dignified. I hate the way everyone keeps harping on her desire to hold on to her privacy now. I respect it totally and I wish others did too. In fact, there are very few things about my mother that I do not admire. Till this day, she is my greatest pillar of strength. Without my mother, I would have turned but to be a completely different person. She instilled in me the importance of keeping a marriage stable and I imbibed it from her. My mother and I are perhaps the only two female stars in films to have begun acting *after* we had mothered our children.

"My mother never ever made me feel the pressure of being her daughter. I cannot say the same for the Bengali film industry though. Mother permitted me to do whatever I wanted to do, she let me play, she encouraged me to paint and draw, I did not miss her much as I was in boarding school and learnt to live independently. I just enjoyed being her daughter and I still do. The only thing she did not wish me to do is to join films. When I announced I was going to do *jatra,* she just freaked out. It was telling on my health at the time. But in the end, she accepted my choice and now, she encourages both my daughters," adds Moon Moon Sen. "The two things she emphasised through my growing up years were—a solid education and a stable family life. I have tried to live up to both. She gave me the best of education one could dream of. I was good at art and she kept one of the best artists to coach me in drawing and painting. And my husband and daughters have given me the happiest moments in my life."

"We have never really idolized our grandmother though she is always around to guide us and show us the way. But for us, they are just mother and grandmother, not Moon Moon Sen and Suchitra Sen. We've never bothered about going along with Ma to her shoots. But we do regret having missed out being on grandma's shoots, we weren't born when she quit," say Raima and Ria.

When asked how she felt about stepping into a Bengali film as leading lady, Raima said, "I felt my flesh tingle and my skin break out in goose pimples when I found myself facing the camera on the same studio floors where my grandmother did such great work in Bengali classics. At certain moments, I just could not believe myself. Tollygunje has a special place in my heart because I am linked to it through blood-ties. At the same time, I understand the disadvantage of being Suchitra Sen's granddaughter. There will be the inevitable comparison I will never be able to live up to." Will

With Sumitra Mukherjee decking her up as a bride

she be able to hold back that unshed tear on her heavy eyelashes before it can drop? Can she break her body language into fragments to express the emotional pain of the character she portrays? Has her grandmother taught her the grammar of expression, body language, look and emotion she had learnt so well? She is in no position to respond to these questions now. For, unlike her reclusive grandmother, she has time on her side.

FILMOGRAPHY

Bengali Films

Name of Film	Director	Actor
1953		
Saat Number Koyedi	Sukumar Dasgupta	Samar Roy
Saarey Chuattor	Nirmal De	Uttam Kumar
Kajori	Niren Lahiri	No hero
Bhagaban Shree Krishna Chaitanya	Debaki Kumar Bose	Basanta Choudhury
1954		
Atom Bomb	Taru Mukhopadhyay	Robin Majumdar
Ora Thaakey Odharey	Sukumar Dasgupta	Uttam Kumar
Dhuli	Pinaki Mukhopadhyay	Prasanta Kumar
Maraner Parey	Satish Dasgupta	Uttam Kumar
Sadanander Mela	Sukumar Dasgupta	Uttam Kumar
Annapunnar Mandir	Naresh Mitra	Uttam Kumar
Agni Pareeksha	Agradoot (Bibhuti Laha)	Uttam Kumar
Griha Prabesh	Ajoy Kar	Uttam Kumar
Balaygras	Pinaki Mukhopadhyay	Uttam Kumar
1955		
Sanjher Pradeep	Sudhangshu Mukherjee	Uttam Kumar
Saajghar	Ajoy Kar	Bikash Roy
Shapmochan	Sudhir Mukherjee	Uttam Kumar
Mejo Bou	Debnarayan Gupta	Bikash Roy

| Bhalobasa | Debaki Kumar Bose | Bikash Roy |
| Sobar Uporey | Agradoot | Uttam Kumar |

1956

Sagarika	Agragami	Uttam Kumar
Subharatri	Sushil Majumdar	Basanta Choudhury
Ekti Raat	Chitto Bose	Uttam Kumar
Trijama	Agradoot	Uttam Kumar
Shilpi	Agragami	Uttam Kumar
Amar Bou	Khagen Roy	Bikash Roy

1957

Harano Sur	Ajoy Kar	Uttam Kumar
Chandranath	Kartik Chatterjee	Uttam Kumar
Pathey Holo Deri	Agradoot	Uttam Kumar
Jiban Trishna	Asit Sen	Uttam Kumar

1958

Raajlakshmi O Sreekanto	Haridas Bhattacharya	Uttam Kumar
Indrani	Niren Lahiri	Uttam Kumar
Suryatoran	Agradoot	Uttam Kumar

1959

| Chawoa Pawoa | Jatrik | Uttam Kumar |
| Deep Jweley Jai | Asit Sen | Basanta Choudhury |

1960

| Hospital | Sushil Majumdar | Ashok Kumar |
| Smriti Tuku Thaak | Jatrik | Bikash Roy, Asit Baran |

1961
Saptapadi   Ajoy Kar   Uttam Kumar

1962
Bipasha   Agradoot   Uttam Kumar

1963
Saat Paakey Bandha   Ajoy Kar   Soumitra Chatterjee
Uttor Phalguni   Asit Sen   Bikash Roy
                                                            Dilip Mukherjee

1964
Sandhya Dweeper Sikha   Haridas Bhattacharya   Bikash Roy

1967
Grihadah   Subodh Mitra   Uttam Kumar
                                                            Pradeep Kumar

1969
Kamallata   Harisadhan Dasgupta   Uttam Kumar

1970
Megh Kalo   Sushil Mukherjee   Basanta Choudhury

1971
Nabaraag   Bijoy Bose   Uttam Kumar
Fariyad   Bijoy Bose   Utpal Dutt

1972
Alo Amar Alo   Pinaki Mukherjee   Uttam Kumar
Haar Mana Haar   Salil Sen   Uttam Kumar

1974

Shraban Sandhya	Chitra Sarathi	Samar Roy
Debi Chaudhurani	Dinen Gupta	Ranjit Mullick

1975

Priyo Bandhabi	Hiren Nag	Uttam Kumar

1976

Datta	Ajoy Kar	Soumitra Chatterjee

1978

Pranoy Pasha	Mangal Chakrabarty	Soumitra Chatterjee

(Filmography has been obtained from the Special Issue of *Television* — Bengali, February, 1993, pp. 52-55, who credited the Filmography to Ramlal Nandi of Chhayabani Pvt. Ltd. and to Pronob Kumar Bosu of Chandimata Films.)

Hindi Films

Name of Film	Actor	Director	Year
Devdas	Dilip Kumar	Bimal Roy	1955
Musafir	Shekhar	H. Mukherjee	1957
Champakali	Bharat Bhushan	Nandlal Jaswantlal	1977
Bambai ka Babu	Dev Anand	Raj Khosla	1960
Sarhad	Dev Anand	Shankar Mukherjee	1960
Mamta	Ashok Kumar	Asit Sen (Bengal)	1966
Aandhi	Sanjeev Kumar	Gulzar	1974

BIBLIOGRAPHY

Phire Phire Chai
by Dhiren Deb
Overland, 1993

Je Jon Aachhen Nirjone
by Suman Gupta
Sukhee Grihokone, 2002

Television Magazine
Aaj Kaal Publications

Smriti, Satta, Suchitra
by Shankarlal Bhattacharya
Anandalok, 2002

Legacy
by Shoma A Chatterji
Verve Magazine, 2001

*I am grateful to
Anshuman Bhowmick
for making archival
documents available to me*

*In a rare moment, clicked by
photographer Tarun Gupta during
the shooting of* Datta